THE CONCISE HISTORIES OF **DEVON**

DEVON AND
THE CIVIL WAR

THE CONCISE HISTORIES OF **DEVON**

DEVON AND
THE CIVIL WAR

MARK STOYLE

Devon during the Civil War

DEVON
AND THE
CIVIL WAR

The English Civil War was the most devastating episode in Devon's recorded history. Between 1642 and 1646 the county was torn apart by violent conflict as town fought against town, village against village and brother against brother. From Ilfracombe in the north to Salcombe in the south, from Axminster in the east to Tavistock in the west, fortifications were built and houses demolished as the tide of war swept, like a blood-red stain, across the land. Thousands of local people lost their lives, thousands more were bereaved or injured, thousands more were robbed of all that they possessed. How did this terrible catastrophe come about?

Most historians agree that - although there were many long-term factors which contributed to the outbreak of the war, and which helped to determine the shape which the conflict eventually took – hostilities would never have broken out in the first place if it had not been for the character and the policies of the reigning monarch: King Charles I. Charles, who acceded to the throne in 1625, was a highly conscientious and principled ruler, but he was also stubborn, reserved and politically maladroit. From the moment that he assumed the Crown, uneasy mutters about the style of his government began to be heard.

Over the next fifteen years, many of the King's subjects became alienated by his high church religious policies and by his apparent determination to rule without the assistance of parliaments. Some, especially the more zealous protestants, or 'puritans', came to believe in the existence of a sinister royal plot:

one which aimed at the restoration of the Catholic faith in England and the destruction of the people's liberties. In 1640, Charles – desperate for cash–at last summoned a Parliament. But instead of financial assistance, he met with angry complaints about his policies. King and Parliament could not agree and during early 1642 England began to divide into two armed camps.

Those who favoured the Parliament were known as 'Roundheads': a reference to the shaven heads of the London apprentices who had been among Parliament's most vociferous supporters during the months which preceded the war. The nickname originated in the capital, quickly spread to the provinces, and was being applied to Parliamentary sympathisers in Devon by as early as April 1642. The king's supporters were known as 'Cavaliers' from the Spanish *Caballeros*, meaning troopers, or armed horsemen. In the West of England, the country-folk frequently shortened this term to 'Cavies' or 'Cabs' and, by the war's end, the ordinary Parliamentary soldier habitually referred to his Royalist opponent as 'Jack Cab'.

In Devon, the leaders of county society were chiefly on Parliament's side, as were the majority of the common people. This owed much to the prevailing religious climate. During the late sixteenth and early seventeenth centuries, zealously protestant ideas had been enthusiastically embraced in many parts of the county: in the cloth-making towns of Tiverton, Collumpton and South Molton, for example, in the ports of Plymouth, Dartmouth and Barnstaple and throughout the length and breadth of North Devon and the South Hams. In these districts, the religious principles of the inhabitants predisposed them to favour the Parliament.

Yet in other parts of the county – most notably the remote parishes around the edge of Dartmoor and the rich arable villages of the Exe Valley – puritanism had failed to establish a foothold and local people had remained conservative in their religious views. By the 1630s, therefore, a major cultural and religious split was developing across Devon between those communities in which puritanism was strong, and those communities which clung to the more traditional ways. The outbreak of the Civil War was to transform this ideological split into an open breach.

THE
COURSE
OF THE
WAR

In July 1642 the Earl of Bath was sent into Devon by Charles I with orders to rally the local community to the Royalist cause. The Earl's presence did little to win opinion over to the King, however. Bath was regarded with suspicion and distrust by most of the county's inhabitants and, although he managed to gain the support of many local gentlemen, his appeals to the common people were contemptuously rebuffed. Bath's popular appeal was so limited, indeed, that his opponents felt able to virtually ignore him. Instead, they turned their attentions to Sherborne Castle in Dorset, which had recently been occupied by a small force of Royalists.

In August a substantial contingent of Devon volunteers marched out of the county to help eject the Cavaliers. According to one eyewitness 'there rose in Devonshire a thousand Horse and Foot' at this time 'that voluntarily went in service against Sherborne'. This impressive display of support for Parliament was quickly followed by the arrest of those few individuals who were still trying to drum up support for the King. Late in September, a troop of Parliamentary horsemen arrived at Tawstock Court, near Barnstaple, to apprehend the Earl of Bath. The Earl – fearful that, if he made any resistance, his magnificent house would be sacked by crowds of vengeful local country-folk – gave himself up without a fight.

Parliamentary dominance of Devon now seemed absolute, but in the neighbouring county of Cornwall it was the Cavaliers who had the whip-hand. In October 1642 ten thousand Cornishmen rose to secure their county for the King. Six weeks later a Cornish Royalist army under Sir Ralph Hopton marched across the Tamar and occupied Tavistock. From here the Cornishmen advanced first to Plymouth – which bade them defiance – and then to Exeter, which they settled down to besiege amid heavy snow and ice. Little had been achieved when news reached Hopton that the Earl of Stamford was marching to Exeter's relief with a Roundhead army.

1643

On New Year's Day 1643 the Cornishmen abandoned their positions before Exeter and trudged back along the snow-filled lanes to Crediton. They were angered by their reverse, and determined to revenge themselves on the inhabitants of Crediton, whom they suspected of favouring the Parliamentary cause. As the ragged Cornish troops passed through the town, they embarked on an orgy of plunder, breaking into houses, and carrying off everything they could lay their hands on. Many of the townsfolk were ruined as a result. Letters reported that Crediton had been 'miserably pillaged by the beggarly Cavaliers', who 'took away the poor people's weaving tools'.

Over the next few days Hopton retreated westwards, closely followed by

Stamford. The Roundhead pursuit proved too impetuous, and on 19 January Hopton turned at bay, defeating a Parliamentary force at Braddock Down in Cornwall. Encouraged by this victory, the Cornishmen invaded Devon again in February, only to be met by massive popular resistance. Some reports spoke of the Parliamentarians having raised 12,000, or even as many as 14,000, men. Their numbers were overwhelming and the Royalists had no choice but to give ground. A truce was agreed upon and Hopton returned to Cornwall.

The temporary cessation of hostilities which followed lasted for two months.

Intensive negotiations took place during March and many local people hoped that some sort of compromise would be agreed upon. Such hopes proved illusory; towards the end of April the cessation expired and conflict was immediately resumed. Three weeks later, Stamford advanced to Stratton in north-east Cornwall with a powerful Parliamentary army. Here, he ordered his men to dig in, confident that his superior numbers would deter any sudden assault. Yet on 16 May his army was attacked and utterly broken by the Royalists. Some 300 Parliamentarians were killed and 1,700 more surrendered: Devon now lay wide open to attack.

Following the victory at Stratton the Royalists marched swiftly through Okehampton, Crediton and Tiverton and on towards the borders of Somerset. Soon afterwards Hopton passed out of Devon altogether, leaving something of a power vacuum behind him. Most of the major towns (Exeter, Plymouth, Dartmouth, Barnstaple and Bideford) were still held for Parliament, as were North Devon and the South Hams. In Central and East Devon, however – the districts in which popular support for the King was strongest – it was the Royalists who were in control. Having summoned in the militia regiments from these areas, and gathered together as many volunteers as they could, the king's local commanders now began a blockade of Exeter.

Over the next three months Devon was riven in two as the rival factions struggled to gain control. Broadly speaking this struggle was waged between the local partisans of King and Parliament. Admittedly, both sides received a certain amount of help from outside the county. Several Royalist regiments were sent back into Devon by Hopton, for example, while the Parliamentary navy brought help to Plymouth and Dartmouth and even attempted to raise the siege of Exeter. By and large though, it was the Devon gentry who directed the conflict during Summer 1643 and the Devon countrymen who supplied the majority of the soldiers.

An effective propaganda campaign helped the king's commanders to build up a sizeable military force at this time. Sufficient men were found to maintain the siege of Exeter and to repel several relief attempts as well. Towards the end of August, moreover, the balance of power in Devon shifted decisively to the King, when 3,000 Cornish soldiers under the command of Charles I's German nephew, Prince Maurice (brother to the more famous Prince Rupert), marched into the county to assist the local Royalists. Within days of their arrival, Barnstaple and Bideford had surrendered. Soon afterwards, Exeter too was given up to the Cavaliers.

From Exeter, Maurice moved against Dartmouth and Plymouth, now the only Devon towns that still remained in Parliamentary hands. Dartmouth was the first to be attacked. The siege of the town lasted for almost a month and Royalist losses were heavy, partly owing to casualties, partly owing to the onset of a virulent strain of fever. Maurice himself lay sick for many weeks, and a clutch of doctors had to be sent for to cure him. Yet

the besiegers persevered, and on 5
October Dartmouth eventually fell.
Maurice could now concentrate his
attentions upon Plymouth and, towards
the end of October, he led a powerful
Royalist army there.

During the next two months the
Royalists suffered a humiliating series of
reverses before the town. Heavy losses
were sustained in repeated frontal assaults
upon the Parliamentary defences and on
Christmas Day 1643 the king's dispirited
army finally withdrew. The great siege of
Plymouth had been an unmitigated
disaster for the Royalists. Hundreds of
their men had been killed and wounded,

and many more were dangerously ill. When the defenders cautiously ventured out to inspect the abandoned Royalist siege-works, they found '660 of the Cavaliers [left] behind sick and maimed and not able to crawl out of their trenches'. Maurice's defeat had shown that the war in the West was not yet lost to Parliament.

1644

Further trouble confronted the Royalists in March 1644, when a serious rebellion broke out in the countryside around Hemyock. This disturbance had been encouraged by the Parliamentary garrison of Lyme Regis, in Dorset, and the Cavaliers decided that the inhabitants of the little fishing port must be punished for their temerity. Accordingly, Maurice brought the full weight of his army to bear upon the town. The siege of Lyme proved as unfortunate for the Prince as the earlier attempt upon Plymouth. The Royalists were unable to penetrate the town defences and again lost many hundreds of men.

By June 1644 Maurice had been beaten to a standstill. When he received word that the Earl of Essex was marching into Dorset with a Parliamentary army, the Prince abandoned the siege and retired to

Exeter. Soon afterwards, he and his forces moved still further west, this time in order to escort Charles I's queen, Henrietta Maria, from Exeter to safety in Cornwall. Meanwhile, Essex had crossed into Devon and occupied Tiverton, where he received an ecstatic welcome. Heartened by his presence, groups of pro-Parliamentarian countrymen – 'Wood-rebels' as the Royalists contemptuously termed them – began to gather in North Devon.

During the next few weeks, the flame of rebellion spread. The townsmen of Barnstaple rose up against their Cavalier masters, as did the inhabitants of Kingsbridge and the surrounding parishes. By mid-July the Royalist position in Devon seemed on the verge of collapse. Yet the arrival of Cavalier reinforcements and the misjudgements of the Parliamentarians quickly transformed the situation. On 20 July Essex took the unwise decision to leave Tiverton and to march still further into the West. Meanwhile, Charles I himself had arrived in Devon with the main Royalist field army. Soon afterwards the King joined Prince Maurice at Exeter.

The combined Royalist armies eventually proved strong enough to defeat the Parliamentary invasion. Essex was trapped at Lostwithiel in Cornwall and his army completely destroyed. Following this signal victory Charles marched back through Devon in triumph, while his troops subdued those parts of the county which had revolted during July. Yet despite these important successes, the King was unable to achieve complete local dominance. Both Plymouth and Lyme continued to hold out for Parliament and their garrisons were to become increasingly bold and disruptive during the ensuing months.

1645

Throughout early 1645 the siege of Plymouth was vigorously prosecuted by the Cornish Royalist general Sir Richard Grenville. But in March Grenville was ordered away. Following his departure, the remaining Royalist troops retired into three large forts which they had built to the north of the town and attempts to take Plymouth by force effectively ceased. Henceforth, it became all the besiegers could do to simply *contain* the Parliamentary garrison. Although relatively secure in their forts, the Royalists now found themselves under virtual siege as the Plymothians sallied forth time and again; attacking vulnerable outposts, capturing local Royalists and carrying off sheep and cattle.

During spring 1645, South Devon was continually troubled by Parliamentarian raids. Similar problems beset the Royalists in East Devon, where the garrison of Lyme was strengthening its grip upon the surrounding countryside. In July local stability disintegrated altogether, when thousands of demoralised Royalist cavalrymen arrived in the county, having been driven out of Somerset by the Parliamentarians. The Royalist horsemen, whose commander, Lord Goring, either would not or could not control them, committed such terrible depredations that bands of armed countrymen –

popularly known as 'Clubmen' – rose up to drive them away.

By September Devon was in a state of near-anarchy, as Clubmen fought Royalists in the North, Royalists fought Plymothians in the South and everyone – Royalist and Parliamentarian alike – did their best to protect themselves from Goring's 'barbarous' Horse. Fortunately for local people, relief was on its way. As the king's cause faltered elsewhere, Sir Thomas Fairfax, the commander of Parliament's New Model Army, had been ordered to reduce the South West, and in October his troops advanced into Devon. Their initial objective was to capture

Exeter and drive the Royalists back into Cornwall but, with winter coming on, Fairfax decided to allow his men some rest. As a result the New Model remained quartered in East Devon throughout late 1645.

1646

In January 1646 the Parliamentarians at last resumed their westward progress. The demoralised Royalist Horse proved utterly unable to stem their advance and were badly defeated in several engagements. Over the next few days, Royalist troops abandoned their positions in South Devon and retreated in confusion towards

the Cornish border. On 13 January the
forces besieging Plymouth withdrew for
the last time and six days later the New
Model Army stormed and captured
Dartmouth. With the South Hams firmly
in Parliamentarian hands, the Royalist
field forces in Devon were now confined
to the north-western corner of the county.

From here, they made one last
attempt to break through to Exeter. In
February, Lord Hopton – recalled, at this
moment of crisis, to supreme command
of the King's Western Army – advanced to
Torrington with all the forces he could
muster, sending a message to Exeter to
expect relief shortly. A few days later, his

army was attacked and defeated by the Parliamentarians in a fierce night battle at Torrington; the Cavalier retreat turning into a rout as their gunpowder magazine, which had been stored in the parish church, exploded above them. Fairfax himself narrowly escaped being killed by the blast.

This was the last major engagement to take place in Devon during the Civil War. Following their defeat the Royalists fled into Cornwall, leaving only a few isolated garrisons behind them. These continued to hold out for some time, pinning their hopes on the king's forces in Cornwall somehow snatching victory from the jaws of defeat. Yet following Hopton's surrender at Truro in March, further resistance became pointless and the surviving garrisons gave themselves up to Parliament one by one. Exeter eventually surrendered in April – Oliver Cromwell, the Lieutenant General of the New Model Army, riding into the city at the head of the Roundhead troops – and by May 1646 the entire county was in Parliamentarian hands. The Civil War in Devon was over.

To reconstruct the course of military events during this period – to trace the progress of the rival armies as they trundled their way, in a ponderous *Danse*

Macabre, across the Devon countryside from battle to siege to storm – is a comparatively straightforward task. Far more difficult is to recapture a sense of what day-to-day existence was like for those who had to live through the conflict; for the ordinary men, women and children of Devon, and for the thousands of strangers who were swept, temporarily, into their midst by the capricious winds of war. How did the Civil War affect all of their lives?

THE
EXPERIENCE
OF
WAR
· MEN ·

Many of the troubles which beset the inhabitants of Devon between 1642 and 1646 afflicted everyone, regardless of their age or sex. All were subject to the myriad fears and insecurities of war; all were exposed to the effects of punitive taxation, to the violence and disorder of the soldiers, and to the ever-present threats of hunger and disease. Disaster sometimes engulfed entire communities. Hundreds were made homeless when the parliamentary garrison of Lyme burnt Axminster to the ground in 1644, and thousands more were cast on the charity of their neighbours when the Royalist garrison of Exeter demolished the city suburbs in order to deny shelter to the advancing New Model Army during the winter of 1645/46. Some of the burdens of war fell almost exclusively upon male shoulders, however – most notably that of military service. How did ordinary men come to find themselves fighting for King or Parliament?

Many, especially in the early months of the war, were volunteers. Some, perhaps the majority, joined up to fight for a cause which they believed in. The Devon men who marched off to besiege Sherborne Castle in 1642 led by a godly minister with a bible in his hand probably saw themselves as engaged on a religious crusade. Others joined up for less high-minded reasons. In 1642, as in 1914, there were many who viewed the war as an exciting adventure, holding out the prospect of escape from humdrum, everyday, lives. Such a one may have been the lad apprehended at Exeter in 1642, who explained to the city magistrates that he had left his job as an apprentice cloth-weaver at Broadhempston in order to go for a volunteer.

Others again were tempted by the money. The wages offered to Civil War foot soldiers – between sixpence and eight pence a day – were not large, but for those whose day-to-day jobs were arduous and poorly paid, the switch from civilian to soldier may well have seemed worth making. Whatever the reasons, there were many who were prepared to enlist voluntarily during the early months of the war. Even so, there were not nearly enough volunteers to go round, and from 1643 onwards both sides increasingly resorted to impressment: that is to say, the raising of soldiers by force.

Needless to say, those who were impressed tended to be the most vulnerable members of contemporary society. Parish constables, faced with the unenviable task of forcing their neighbours to fight for King or Parliament, naturally chose those who possessed the least local influence: the poor, the marginal and the unruly. John Palmer of Halberton, who served as a wartime constable, later testified that those whom he had taken up to serve for the King were 'for the most part such as were regardless of themselves and such who lived a kind of an idle life'. When such men could not be had, however, the constables would press almost anyone they could get.

Some constables, driven on by partisan zeal or fear of punishment, would go to almost any lengths to persuade the unwilling to enlist. William Hookway, constable of Broadhembury, was later said to have 'violently ... impressed many and bound and forcibly carried them to the King's forces, and hunted others violently, besetting their houses with Horse and Foot, so that they had to live in dens, caves, woods, etc and durst not come near their families, whereby they were almost famished'. Another constable, Thomas Jope of Buckland, allegedly 'acted most cruelly ... by forcing ... [men] into chests, ovens and chimneys to compel them to fight for the King'.

Should the constables' best efforts fail, the military themselves would take on the role of man-hunters; with groups of soldiers scouring town and countryside alike for able-bodied men. Even at church, people were not safe from the press-gang. Francis Drewe of Newton Ferrers later recalled that a Royalist lieutenant 'with a party of soldiers of the King's Army upon a Lord's Day did put a guard upon the church-doors of Newton Ferrers and as this deponent came forth of the church, the said lieutenant laid hold on him and swore that he should serve the King'. Several other church-goers were press-ganged at the same time.

Once a man was in the army, it was very hard for him to get out again. There were possible methods, of course. Parents sometimes managed to bribe the constables to release their sons, while those who had contacts in high places might also have a chance of being spared. James Eveleigh, a Devon gentlemen, wrote to the Royalist Commissioners in 1643, explaining that Anthony Clap 'our ... workman ... is now pressed' and that 'I desire humbly his releasement, [he] having a wife and 2 or 3 children which are like to be my charge'.

For those with no money or contacts, the only way to get out of the army was to desert. This was not an easy option, as the punishments for desertion were harsh, and most regiments kept lists of the parishes from which their soldiers came, meaning that those deserters who ran home could easily be picked up again. Even so, many thousands did desert – and the fact that they were prepared to run the risk of doing so hints at just how bad conditions in the army must have been.

Today the Civil War tends to be regarded as a rather gentlemanly combat, but contemporary testimony quickly destroys this illusion, reminding us that warfare in the seventeenth century was just as brutal and bloody as it has always been. Take the story of Nathaniel Jefford, a husbandman of Dunsford, who served in the King's Army under Major Francis Fulford:

'from the very beginning of the ... rebellion until the end thereof, and was ... a corporal ... and in the said service received many wounds and first at Weymouth was shot in the shoulder and at Hill Bishops [near Taunton] was shot in the neck and knocked in the back of the head with a stock of a musket and was left for dead ... and was ... taken ... to ... Exeter and ... kept a close prisoner [for] 17 weeks and underwent much hardship and cruelty and by the wound in his neck ... lost the liberty of his speech, which has been imperfect ever since'.

Thousands of other Devon men could have told similar stories of wounding and imprisonment – and of course they were the lucky ones. For all too many Civil War soldiers, the 'great adventure' ended in death. One of the very few whose last moments were recorded in detail was the Royalist Captain George Cloberry, of Bradstone. While serving in the King's army before Plymouth in 1645 Clobbery learnt that a force of Parliamentarians had sallied forth from the town. Accordingly, 'he forthwith sounded to Horse with great resolution to defeat them, but riding on too hastily, before his troop could follow him, two [Roundhead] soldiers that lay in Ambush … [near] Boringdon House … fired at him both at once, and shot him off his horse'.

Clobbery was 'much wounded', but might still have survived had his attackers not then 'taken him, and tying their match [i.e. match-cord] to his heels, dragged him after them, with his head dashing on the ground, until … almost dead, they carried him into … Plymouth in triumph'. Poor Clobbery died soon afterwards. His brother, John – who, by a cruel twist of fate, had chosen to support the opposing side and was serving as an officer in the Roundhead garrison– demanded that the two soldiers be court-martialled. Tried and 'found guilty of murdering their prisoners', they were 'deservedly shot to death'. Had their victim not been a well-connected local gentleman, the killers might well have escaped unpunished.

THE
EXPERIENCE
OF
WAR
· WOMEN ·

I t was men who did most of the fighting, but it should not be thought that women were indifferent to the political issues of the day. On the contrary, they frequently displayed the most passionate concern. In one North Devon town in September 1642, a crowd of women scratched the face of a Royalist gentleman when he attempted to persuade their husbands to support the King. When the

Earl of Bath and his gentry allies rode into South Molton on a similar mission a few days later, they found that the women of the town 'had filled the steps of the [town] cross with great stones, and got up and sat on them, swearing if they [i.e. the Royalists] did come there, they would brain them all'. One woman, a butcher's wife, even 'came running with her lap full of rams horns' to throw at the luckless Earl.

Crowds of women were most likely to be stirred to anger by particular threats to their local communities. When Sir Alexander Carew attempted to betray Plymouth to the Royalists in 1643, an angry mob of townswomen 'fell upon him, and would have beaten out his brains, if the mayor ... had not rescued him'. Similarly, when the Cavalier garrison of Dartmouth surrendered to the New Model Army in 1646, the Royalist 'engineer' – who had been in charge of overseeing and extending the town defences – 'was in danger to have been torn in pieces by the women of the town, for his cruelty in burning of houses and other villainous acts'.

On a number of occasions, women ventured into the very thick of the fighting. Evidence from elsewhere in the country reveals that a handful of exceptional women bore arms and fought alongside the men during the Civil War, and there may well have been such female warriors – 'she soldiers', as they were known to contemporaries – in Devon. A woman named Hester Parramoore certainly served as a gunner in the Parliamentary fort of Mount Gould, near Plymouth, in 1645. Other possible female combatants from Devon include Florence Abatha, one of the eleven local people who are recorded to have been slain in a fight between the inhabitants of Ilfracombe and a party of Royalist horsemen in August 1644, and 'Katharine Trevanion, a Cavalier', one of the many

Royalists who were buried at Plymouth during 1645, and who may well have been killed in the fighting around the town.

Many women who did not take up arms themselves nevertheless played a vital role in defending their communities against attack. During the Royalist siege of Lyme, it was observed that 'the women of the town would come into the thickest of the danger to bring powder, bullets and provisions to the men', and encourage them in the trenches. Similarly, at the siege of Plymouth, the townswomen brought out 'strong waters [i.e. alcoholic spirits], and all sorts of provisions in the midst of … [the fighting] for refreshing of … [the] soldiers, though many [were] shot through the clothes' as they made their way to the front line. As well as being extremely dangerous, these journeys under fire exposed women to all sorts of gruesome sights. One poor soul, who was taking up a parcel of food to a relative serving in the outworks at Plymouth, met with his headless corpse being carried back into the town, slung across the saddle of a horse.

Lugging supplies to the front line was only one of the ways in which the women of Devon provided assistance to the fighting men. They helped to construct fortifications: at Exeter, Plymouth,

Dartmouth and Barnstaple, and probably at many other places besides. They lent money and gave gifts to their party of choice. And above all, in every corner of the county, they looked after the ordinary soldiers: lodging them, feeding them and nursing them when they were ill. During the siege of Exeter in Summer 1643, Agnes Trust and Mary Squire were reimbursed by the Parliamentary treasurer of Devon for tending to the sick soldiers of the garrison there, while two years later a certain Elizabeth Hixe was paid 16 shillings by the Parliamentary authorities in Plymouth 'for attending diverse soldiers of Captain Calmady's in their sickness, & for necessaries for them'.

Some local women provided the soldiers with altogether more personal services: whether through choice or compulsion is not always clear. Major Alexander Balfour was an officer in the Cavalier army besieging Plymouth during the winter of 1644/45. In December 1644 his wife, Joan, fell ill and died at the Royalist headquarters at Plympton. Balfour sought comfort in the arms of a local girl, one Philippa Gosse, and, as she herself later testified, 'had frequent use of her body for 6 weeks together ... in Plympton St Mary about ... Easter ... 1645'. Philippa duly became pregnant, but by the time she went into labour – in the bleak month of January 1646 – her lover had fled along with the rest of the besiegers, and she and her illegitimate child were left to face the condemnation of the local community alone.

A number of women accompanied the soldiers on campaign. Behind the rival armies there marched tatterdemalion bands of female camp-followers – some of them soldiers' wives or lovers, some of them ladies of more doubtful virtue – whom the coarser Cavaliers termed 'Camp-bitches'. The lives of these women were hard and uncertain. Many lost their male protectors through accident of war and found themselves left penniless, alone and far from home. One such was Mary Parnell, of Barnstaple, who was brought before a magistrate in February 1645 and accused of stealing a coat. Denying the charge, Mary explained that she had bought the coat from 'a trooper in the Highway about two miles southward from Great Torrington, she coming that way homeward from Plympton ... her husband being lately killed in fight against Plymouth'.

Hundreds, probably thousands of Devon women were widowed during the Civil War, and were left to scratch a living for themselves as best they could. For those whose husbands had died in active service, there was sometimes a paltry one-off payment from the local military authorities. When Alice Stripling's husband died fighting for Parliament in Exeter in 1643, for example, she received 10 shillings towards 'the charges of [his] burial', while three other women whose husbands were killed in the same service were awarded the princely sum of £1 apiece. Such extraordinary payments aside, soldiers' widows were supposed to receive a regular pension from a central fund administered by the county magistrates. As the number of war-widows soared, however, demand for pensions outstripped the money which was available to fund them. By early 1644, desperate appeals were regularly being made in Devon churches for 'collecting of monies towards the maintenance of distressed widows whose husbands have been slain in the wars'.

Many widows failed to secure any sort of pension at all, and the plight of such individuals is well summed up in a petition which was sent to the judges of the Western Circuit by Joan Evans, Elizabeth Ball and Alice Worth of Plymouth in 1649. The three women complained 'that your poor petitioners for these many years have been in extreme want, and lived in great misery, by reason their husbands were all slain in the late war in the defence of this town, leaving to each of your poor petitioners three or four small children, who are not able to help themselves, neither have [they] any help from any others, except from your poor petitioners, which is very small, God knows'.

THE
EXPERIENCE
OF
WAR
· CHILDREN ·

This petition serves as a reminder that the children of Devon were also grievously affected by the conflict. Thousands lost one or both parents between 1642 and 1646, hundreds more saw their homes destroyed, while many others found themselves forced into temporary exile with their families. Even those who were fortunate enough to escape the worst consequences of war had their lives turned upside down. Naturally, the wartime experiences of children are less well documented than are those of adults. Nevertheless a good deal of information has survived.

We know, for example, that children had their schooling disrupted. George Trobridge of Thorverton later recalled that he had 'had a licence to teach school' in the village, and had taught nearly 40 children there, until, in 1644 'the Earl of Essex came into Thorverton and routed master, scholars and all'. We know, too, that the war made such a vivid impression on children that it intruded itself into their games. At Southampton, in

Hampshire, the boys of the town divided themselves up into rival gangs of Roundheads and Cavaliers and whooped through the streets fighting mock battles. Similar games were enjoyed by Devonian children. During the siege of Plymouth, in 1644, a group of townsfolk attending a religious service heard loud noises just outside the church and voices shouting 'Arms! Arms!'. The service at once broke up in confusion and the men in the congregation issued forth 'with their swords drawn' to deal with the emergency – only to find that the noise had been caused by a group of children playing outside.

Sometimes the play was less innocent. When a group of imprisoned Royalist clergymen were marched through the streets of Exeter by the Parliamentarians in 1643 they were 'blasted, and abused, and hooted at' by local boys, who also threw 'dirt' at the discomforted captives. Like Samuel Pepys, who later recalled that 'I was a great Roundhead when I was a boy', these lads clearly knew which side they supported. It seems probable that most Devon children did. Certainly, they followed the war's progress, and discussed its events with those around them. In 1644, for example, the children of an Exeter shop-keeper are known to have fallen into conversation with two men who came into their father's shop about 'the report that was then in the … city of the routing of [the Parliamentary] forces'. In emergencies, children sometimes turned out to help to defend their communities. At Plymouth and Exeter, boys and girls laboured on the town defences, just as men and women did, while at South Molton in 1642 children, as well as men and women, armed themselves with makeshift weapons to resist the Earl of Bath.

Many boys were to be found in the baggage train of the rival armies. Most were presumably the dependents of the soldiers, or of female camp-followers, while others were employed as servants. These youngsters performed many useful tasks around the camp. Some helped to look after the horses, for example – these individuals were known as 'horse-boys' or 'padees' – while others foraged for supplies. As they grew older, many of the camp boys probably graduated to fighting alongside the soldiers. Officially, it was only men between the ages of 16 and 60 who could be called upon to perform military service, but some of those who fought in Devon were undoubtedly younger.

Captain Chichester Wrey, of Trebigh

in Cornwall, was just 15 years old when he was captured by the Parliamentarians at the battle of Sourton Down, near Okehampton in April 1643. Fortunately for Wrey, his captors paid him little attention, 'thinking him to be but a trooper's boy', and he was soon able to make his escape. A year later, he was commissioned as a Colonel in the Royalist army. The Parliamentarians, for their part, appear to have committed many boy-soldiers to action. At the height of the siege of Plymouth in 1643, a Roundhead correspondent admitted that much of the hardest fighting around the town was being done by 'those poor little boys (for the most part of them are such)', who had recently been shipped down from London under the command of Colonel William Gould.

STRANGERS

Gould's youthful Londoners were by no means the only 'foreign' troops to arrive in Devon between 1642 and 1646. One of the most disturbing consequences of the Civil War, as far as the ordinary inhabitants of Devon were concerned, was that it led to an unprecedented influx of 'vurriners'. Men and women from every corner of England poured into Devon with the rival armies –

thousands of 'Cocknies' with the Earl of Essex in 1644, for example, thousands of Midlanders with the King later that year, and hundreds of battle-hardened Northerners with Lord Goring in 1645.

There were few districts, if any, to which these visitors did not penetrate, and Devon parish registers recorded the burials of scores of lonely exiles; including 'John, a London soldier' who was buried at Buckland Brewer in 1643, 'Thomas Slopen, a soldier which came from Shropshire' who was buried at Exminster in March 1645 and 'Henry Boose, a soldier … [and] a Lancashire man' who was hanged at Torrington for mutiny a few months later. Nor was it only from other parts of England that people flooded in, for the county witnessed the arrival of hordes of 'strangers' (i.e. non-English folk) as well.

Most ubiquitous were the Cornish soldiers, some of them still speaking the ancient Celtic tongue of their forefathers, who had rallied to Charles I's standard in such numbers at the beginning of the war. It was the Cornishmen who had conquered Devon for the King in 1643, and thereafter Cornish troops remained active throughout the entire county: helping to maintain the Royalist siege of Plymouth, bolstering the garrisons of

Royalist-held towns like Exeter and Dartmouth and manning a number of smaller Royalist positions, like the forts at Appledore and Exmouth.

In July 1645 a sizeable contingent of Welsh infantrymen – who had been shipped across the Bristol Channel to join Lord Goring's army – also arrived in Devon. (The 'strange Welsh woman' who was shot dead by a soldier at Ilfracombe soon afterwards was presumably one of their camp-followers). These Welsh-speaking troops remained in the county throughout the winter of 1645/46 – and it would be intriguing to know if they struck up links with the Cornish Royalist soldiers who served alongside them and whose Celtic language and culture was so similar to their own.

To the inhabitants of seventeenth-century Devon, the Cornish and – to a lesser extent – the Welsh were the closest of foreigners: undeniably different from the English, yet at the same time reassuringly familiar. Even so, the presence of large numbers of Cornish and Welsh troops in the county aroused considerable resentment, while the arrival of parties of armed 'strangers' from still further afield caused genuine alarm. After 200 Scottish mercenaries, driven into Plymouth by contrary winds, joined the

Roundhead garrison there in 1642, local Royalists informed their neighbours that the Parliamentarians 'intended to settle an Army of Scottish soldiers in those parts … [to] keep that … [county] in subjection': a rumour which was widely believed. The Roundheads, for their part, assured everyone who would listen that the Royalist forces were full of murderous Irish Catholics, eager to wash their hands in English blood. Such black propaganda led to several unfortunate Irish Royalist soldiers (of whom there were, in fact, very few in Devon) being put to death the moment they were captured – as happened at Fitzford House, near

Tavistock, in 1644.

Almost as hated as the Irish, and probably even more feared, were the soldiers of fortune who had made their way to England from the Continent. At the beginning of the Civil War there were only a handful of such 'outlanders' in Devon, most of them employed as military advisers, but as time went by their numbers steadily increased, especially on the Royalist side. Frenchmen, Dutchmen, Germans, Spaniards, Italians, Swedes and Danes are all known to have fought in Devon during the conflict.

One group of foreign mercenaries who sparked off particular local outrage were the French troopers of Queen Henrietta Maria's regiment of horse, who were said to be 'notorious ravishers'. Having escorted their pregnant royal mistress to Exeter in May 1644, these unwelcome visitors settled down to quarter in the countryside around Cullompton, from where it was soon being reported that the inhabitants 'generally cry out at the pressures and abuses of the French Horse'. When the Queen – by now safely delivered of a daughter – set off for Cornwall two months later her regiment accompanied her, spreading panic across the north and west of Devon.

The inhabitants of Barnstaple feared that, if the French troopers managed to gain admittance to their town, they would burn it to the ground. The Cornish soldiers guarding the bridges along the Tamar appear to have been equally suspicious of the Frenchmen's proclivities. According to the Parliamentarians, they permitted the Queen herself to pass into Cornwall, but refused to admit 'the nasty, thievish … buggering, beastly French … of her Majestie's Dark Guard'. As a result, the dreaded troopers were forced to remain behind in Devon. This particular contingent of Frenchmen left the West

Country a few months later, but when Goring fell back into Devon in summer 1645 he brought with him an entire 'French Brigade', consisting of three separate regiments of horse.

The last year of the Civil War saw Devon positively awash with 'strangers' fighting in the King's service: the Danish cavalry commander Lord Muller, for example, who had established his headquarters in East Devon by early 1645; the (French or Spanish?) 'Captain de Consull' whose cavalry troop was billeted at Colyton in March; the 'gentleman of France', a volunteer in the King's army, who was buried in Exeter Cathedral in

May, the Italian Major Cosmo Manucci who was captured by the Parliamentarians at Tiverton Castle in October; and the anonymous Dutch Captain who was slain by a Roundhead raiding party at Staverton in that same month.

Alongside such high-ranking individual foreigners as these, the King's Western Army included an unknown number of Irishmen, a sprinkling of mercenary troopers from the continent, some 400-500 Welsh foot soldiers and perhaps as many as 5,000 Cornishmen. It is easy to see why Roundhead propagandists jeered that 'his Majesty's Army – [is] a tyrannical medley of all nations', and why the people of Devon, terrified by the swelling number of 'outlanders' in their midst, eventually greeted Parliament's New Model Army – which was composed almost entirely of native-born Englishmen – with open arms.

AFTERMATH

What happened after the Civil War was over? At the national level, Parliament's military victory was to have momentous political consequences. Although desperate attempts were made to arrive at a permanent peace settlement between 1646 and 1648, Charles I – now, in effect, a prisoner of the Parliament – was not prepared to play along. Oliver Cromwell and other senior officers of the New Model Army eventually grew thoroughly exasperated with the royal captive, and in January 1649 Charles I was put on trial for his life, found guilty and publicly executed. Eleven years of Republican rule followed – but in 1660 the 'Martyr King's' son, Charles II, returned to England and the monarchy was restored.

For the people of Devon the post-war period was a time of great hardship. Everywhere, there were people who had been ruined, or crippled, or bereaved, or made homeless by the war. The conflict had devastated the county, and for many years after 1646 the ruinous activities of the rival armies were memorialised in the scars which remained vividly inscribed upon the Devon landscape; in the ruins of demolished bridges, for example; in the charred shells of churches, almshouses and hospitals; in the 'dunghills and heaps of ashes' which were all that was left to mark the sites of formerly prosperous suburban streets; and in the string of blackened, burnt-out mansion houses which littered the countryside around Plymouth and Lyme – Ashe House, Boringdon House, Colcombe House, Ham House, Shute Barton and Stedcombe House, to name just a few.

The buildings destroyed during the Civil War often took decades to be rebuilt: Axminster did not recover to its pre-war extent until the late 1660s, while, at Exeter, houses were still being constructed to replace those which had been demolished during the Civil War in 1713 – nearly 70 years after the conflict had come to an end!

The physical scars of the Civil War were remarkably enduring, then. But what of the mental scars which accompanied them? Although most local people tried to put their wartime experiences behind them after 1646, some found it impossible to do so. Ex-

Cavaliers and Roundheads continued to regard each other with resentment and dislike for decades to come – and from time to time the old divisions resurfaced. During the Monmouth Rebellion of 1685 some of the East Devon men who flocked to join the 'Protestant Duke' in his doomed attempt to oust Charles I's son from the throne were 'Old Oliverians': men who had fought for Parliament during the Civil War, and who regarded Monmouth as the new champion of the 'Good Old [Parliamentary] Cause'. On the other side, there were still old men in Devon as late as 1705 who took pride in the fact that they had fought and suffered in the army of 'King Charles I of Blessed Memory'. The Civil War did not truly come to an end, it might almost be said, until all of those who had fought in it were dead.

And even after the generation of the 1640s had passed away the events of the Civil War were not entirely forgotten for they passed down into folklore, legend and myth. Lord Goring's Royalist plunderers were still remembered with abhorrence during the eighteenth century. Indeed their memory spawned a dialect term: 'a Goring's Crew', meaning a drunken, disorderly rabble.

In 1708 an Exeter preacher referred, with a thrill of horror, to 'the rapes, barbarities and outrages of Goring's Crew', and added that 'for their horrid villainies [they are] infamous to this day through all the West of England'. Songs about Goring and his 'cursed crew' were still being sung during the 1790s, and as late as 1852 a correspondent from Morwenstow (just over the border from Devon, in north-east Cornwall) could report to a London journal that '[here] a rude, rough roisterer is called, to this day, a Goring'.

There could be no better illustration of the enormous impact that the events of the Civil War had had upon West-Country folk. They had lived through a nightmare; it was one which was to haunt their dreams for centuries to come.

FURTHER READING

There are four major studies of Devon in the Civil
War: R.W. Cotton, *Barnstaple and the Northern Part of
Devonshire during the Great Civil War* (London, 1889);
E.A. Andriette, *Devon and Exeter in the Civil War*
(Newton Abbot, 1971); Mark Stoyle, *Loyalty and
Locality: Popular Allegiance in Devon during the English
Civil War* (Exeter, 1994); and Mark Stoyle, *From
Deliverance to Destruction: Rebellion and Civil War in an
English City* (Exeter, 1996).

In addition, there are a number of smaller books
and articles. The most important of these are: J.
Davidson, *Axminster in the Civil War* (Axminster,

1851); R.N. Worth, 'The Siege of Plymouth', *Report and Transactions of the Plymouth Institute*, 5 (1875-76), pp. 250-311; A.C. Miller, 'The Impact of the Civil War in Devon', *Transactions of the Devonshire Association*, 104 (1972), pp. 149-74; S. Porter, 'The Destruction of Axminster in 1644', *Devon and Cornwall Notes and Queries*, 35 (1985), pp. 243-246; I.R. Palfrey, 'Devon and the Outbreak of the English Civil War, 1642-43', *Southern History*, 10 (1988), pp. 29-46; E. Besly, 'The Exeter Mint, 1643-46', *Devon Archaeological Society Proceedings*, 50 (1992), pp. 91-115; and S.K. Roberts, 'War and Society in Devon, 1642-46', *Transactions of the Devonshire Association*, 127 (1995), pp. 81-96.

Silver crown struck by the Royalists at Exeter in 1645
(by courtesy of Exeter Museums Service)

Also available in the Concise Histories of Devon Series

Roman Devon	Malcolm Todd
The Vikings and Devon	Derek Gore
Elizabethan Devon	Todd Gray

Also by **The Mint Press**

The Devon Engraved Series

Exeter Engraved: The Secular City (2000)

Exeter Engraved: The Cathedral, Churches, Chapels and Priories (2001)

Devon Country Houses and Gardens Engraved (2001)

Dartmoor Engraved (2001)

The Travellers' Tales Series

Exeter (2000)

East Devon (2000)

Cornwall (2000)